Mok

Rivers and Valleys

Philip Sauvain

 Carolrhoda Books, Inc. / Minneapolis

All words that appear in **bold** are explained in the glossary that starts on page 30.

Photographs courtesy of: © Aerofilms of Borehamwood for Durham Cathedral 15b; Cephas Picture Library / E.Bischof 22; Mary Evans Picture Library 16; The Hutchison Library / Patricia Goycoolea 12; / John Downman 13; / Lesley Nelson 17b; / Amon Frank 20t; / Andrew Eames 24b; Impact Photos / Colin Jones 9; / Piers Cavendish 25t; John Mills Photography Ltd., Liverpool 8; Willard Price / National Geographic Image Collection 19b; Robert Harding Picture Library / Robin Scagell 20b; Philip A. Sauvain 7t, 10, 11t & b, 19t, 23, 27t, 28; South American Pictures / Tony Morrison 5, 7b, 26br; Frank Spooner Pictures 17t; Zefa - title page, 15t, 24t, 25b, 26t & bl, 27b.

Illustrations by David Hogg. Maps by Gecko Limited.

The extract on page 16 is taken from *An American Doctor's Odyssey* by Victor Heiser, W. W. Norton, Inc., quoted in *Splendor of Earth*, ed. Margaret S. Anderson, George Philip & Son Ltd., 1954.

This edition first published in the United States in 1996 by Carolrhoda Books, Inc.

A ZOË BOOK

Copyright © 1995 Zoë Books Limited. Originally produced in 1995 by Zoë Books Limited, Winchester, England.

Carolrhoda Books, Inc., c/o The Lerner Group
241 First Avenue North, Minneapolis, MN 55401

Library of Congress Cataloging-in-Publication Data

Sauvain, Philip Arthur.
    Rivers and valleys / Philip Sauvain; [illustrations by David Hogg; maps by Gecko Limited].
        p. cm. — (Geography Detective)
    "A Zoë book" — T.p. verso.
    Includes index.
    Summary: Text and illustrations, with questions and activities, provide information about rivers and such related topics as valleys, waterfalls, dams, and floods.
    ISBN 0-87614-996-4
        1. Rivers — Juvenile literature. 2. Valleys — Juvenile literature.
    [1. Rivers.] I. Hogg, David, 1943- ill. II. Gecko Ltd.
    III. Title. IV. Series.
    GB1203.8.S28 1996
    551.48'3 — dc20   95-17369
                                                            CIP
                                                             AC

Printed in Italy by Grafedit SpA.
Bound in the United States of America
1 2 3 4 5 6 01 00 99 98 97 96

Contents

Draining the Land

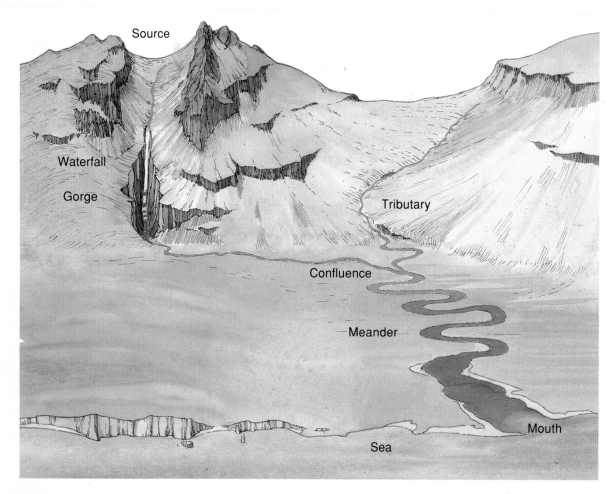

Source

Waterfall

Gorge

Tributary

Confluence

Meander

Mouth

Sea

▲ The start of each river is its **source**, which may be a lake or a **spring** high up on the side of a hill. Rivers that join a main river are **tributaries**. The place where they meet is called a **confluence**. A river ends at its **mouth**. This is the point where the river enters the sea, a lake, or a larger river. Underground streams may join the river. They come to the surface as springs. The rivers flowing into one main river are part of its **drainage system**. The area of land they drain is a **drainage basin**.

Rivers always flow downhill. When rivers are full of water, they cut into, or **erode**, the earth to carve out valleys. They wash the eroded earth and rocks downstream, but only as far as the flow of the river allows. Heavy rocks, stones, and pebbles cannot be carried far. Small pieces, or particles, of sand and mud are very light and are easily carried the length of the river.

The amount of water that drains into the river system depends partly on how quickly the rainwater dries in the sun. Some water soaks into the soil and rocks. This underground water may join the river later from a spring.

▶ The Amazon River is close to the **equator**, where the climate is very hot and very wet. The heat and moisture create thick evergreen forests, called tropical rainforests, throughout much of the Amazon drainage basin.

● The world's longest rivers are the Nile (4,145 mi) in Africa, the Amazon (4,000 mi) in South America, and the Chang (3,915 mi) in China.

● The Mississippi (2,340 mi) is the longest river in North America. Europe's is the Volga (2,194 mi).

● Other very long rivers are the Huang (2,903 mi) and the Mekong (2,600 mi) in Asia, and the Congo (2,900 mi) and the Niger (2,600 mi) in Africa.

The Amazon is the most powerful river in the world. It carries much more water to the sea than any other river. Some of its water comes from melting snow in the Andes mountains. Most of the water comes from tropical rainfall in the Amazon rainforest. The Amazon's drainage basin covers an area of about 270,000 square miles — more than two-thirds the size of the United States.

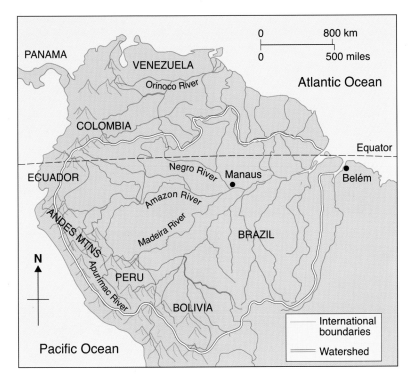

◀ This map shows the drainage basin of the Amazon River. The line that separates the Amazon drainage system from its neighbors, such as the Orinoco, is called a **watershed**.

Geography Detective

Find these features on the map of the Amazon drainage system: a source of the Amazon; the mouth of the river; the name of a tributary; a confluence.

The Source and Uses of a River

When rain falls, some water seems to dry up, or **evaporate** into the air. Some water sinks into the ground, and the rest is called **runoff**. It drains into a valley, a lake, or a watery area such as a marsh or swamp, called a **wetland**. The water that sinks into the ground may reach the surface later on as a spring from an underground stream. Some of the runoff comes from melting snow and ice.

▼ This diagram shows how water from the sea evaporates to form clouds. It later falls as rain, which rivers take back to the sea. Because this process is repeated over and over again it is called the **water cycle**.

The moisture in the air is called water vapor. It is invisible except when it forms clouds of tiny droplets.

As the clouds rise, they get cooler and the water droplets merge and begin to fall as rain, hail, sleet, or snow. This is called precipitation.

RUNOFF

RUNOFF

River

Sea

Some precipitation sinks into the ground. Most of the rest drains into rivers and streams and flows toward a lake or the sea. This surface water is called runoff.

● Some great rivers separate one country from another. Part of the frontier between Switzerland and Germany and between France and Germany follows the Rhine River. The St. Lawrence forms part of the border between the United States and Canada. The Paraná separates Brazil from Paraguay in South America. The Zambezi forms the frontier between Zambia and Zimbabwe in Africa. The Mekong separates Thailand from Laos in Asia.

▶ The source of a river is often little more than a hole or hollow in the ground, high up on the slope of a hill or mountain. Two hundred feet lower down the hillside, the hollow has already widened to become the valley of a small stream.

Streams and rivers have many uses. They may supply fresh water to people who live near them. Farmers may use rivers to water, or **irrigate**, their crops. The power of the moving water in rivers and streams may be used to turn waterwheels. Waterpower can also drive machines that make **hydroelectricity**. In some countries, rivers are used to get rid of waste materials. Boats and barges carry people and goods along rivers.

Geography Detective

The Apurímac River valley, seen here, is close to the source of the Amazon River in the Andes Mountains. Melting snow and ice help to swell the flow of this tributary high in the Andes. About 4,000 miles downstream, the river enters the Atlantic Ocean.

How does a river like this affect the places where people live and work? How do they travel? Where do they build their homes?

The Mouth of a River

◀ This photograph shows the Mersey Estuary at Liverpool, England. Many of the world's greatest ports are on the shores of an estuary like this one. Hamburg is on the Elbe in Germany, Buenos Aires is on the Río de la Plata in Argentina, and Baltimore is on the shores of the Chesapeake Bay in the United States.

A river usually gets much wider as it reaches the sea. At high tide, the sea rushes upstream, while at low tide it retreats. The sea and the river carry with them the mud and sand, called **sediment**, brought down by the river. In this way, the tidal stretch of a river, its **estuary**, is cleared of sediment by the actions of the river and ocean tides. Tidal action makes the waterway suitable for ships.

There are no tides where a river enters a lake. This is why mud and other **deposits** pile up at the river mouth. They spread out into the lake in the shape of a fan, or **delta**. A delta may also form when a river enters the sea. The mud deposits break up the flow of the river water into many smaller channels. Ships can sail through large river deltas, such as the Nile and the Mississippi.

● Some rivers just dry up. They end in a desert or in an inland river basin with no outlet to the sea. In the Middle East, the Jordan River flows into the Dead Sea. This inland river basin is 1,300 feet below sea level.

● The Ganges River in Bangladesh has the world's biggest delta. Other large deltas include those of the Mississippi and the Rhine.

● Tidal action in the estuary of the Rance in France is so strong it can be used to generate electricity. The world's first tidal power station was completed here in 1966.

The Mississippi delta is a maze of channels running through mud banks and swamps. These channels are called **distributaries**. Today the delta is shrinking in size. The flow of the river is falling, and it is carrying less mud and sand downstream.

▼ This photograph shows part of the Mississippi delta as seen from the air.

Geography Detective

Trace or copy this diagram. It shows how a delta is made up of layer upon layer of mud or sand. These layers extend the mouth of the river into the lake. Add extra layers of mud to your picture. Show what you think will eventually happen to the lake if the river continues to bring down mud for thousands of years.

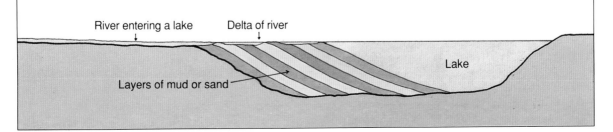

River entering a lake   Delta of river
↓   ↓

Layers of mud or sand

Lake

How Rivers Cut their Valleys

◀ The sheer force of the water in a river is not enough to cut a deep valley. But when the water carries with it boulders, stones, and pebbles, it can cut through earth and rock. This is why the stones and rocks on the river bed are called the tools of the river.

Rivers are most powerful when they are brimful of water after days of heavy rain or melting snow. The river surges forward, causing havoc when it destroys bridges and embankments. The force of the river armed with stones and pebbles cuts down into the river bed. Sometimes the surging water carves out or deepens a **waterfall**. In other places it

● The power of a river to deepen and widen its valley depends on the amount of water it carries. This river flow, as it is called, can vary widely from river to river. It is at its greatest when the river banks hold the largest amount of water possible without overflowing.

● On average, the Amazon carries 60 times as much water to the sea as the world's longest river — the Nile in Africa.

▼ These diagrams show how a valley changes shape as a river cuts into its bed and erodes its banks. As the river swings from side to side, it widens the valley floor and undercuts the valley sides.

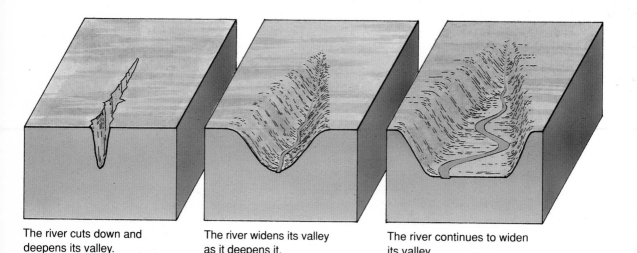

The river cuts down and deepens its valley.

The river widens its valley as it deepens it.

The river continues to widen its valley.

may form a deep **gorge**. If the water swirls the stones round and round in one place, they will scrape out a **pothole**. The photograph below shows how a river can cut down into its bed. Acting like a power drill, the river makes the potholes wider and deeper.

Slowly, the sides of the valley are widened, too. The weather plays a part in this. It helps break up the rocks on the valley slopes. Water in cracks in the rocks freezes and breaks off sharp fragments. Some rocks break apart when the weather is wet and very hot. Heavy rain makes the ground soggy. Earth slides downhill, sometimes as a massive landslide, or avalanche. The river carries the weathered rocks and soil away. This is why a river in flood is discolored. Eroded materials dissolve in the water and make it change color.

▲ This mountain stream is full of water after heavy rain. The gray color comes from the loose sediment that the stream has eroded from the valley sides. When the water level falls, the river will no longer have the power to carry materials downstream. The dirt will settle to the bottom and the water will become clear again.

Geography Detective

Draw a picture of the potholes in the photograph. Add labels and arrows to explain how a pothole is formed. What will happen to the river bed when the potholes get deeper and wider?

Waterfalls and Gorges

▼ Waterfalls are often formed where hard rock lies on top of softer rock.

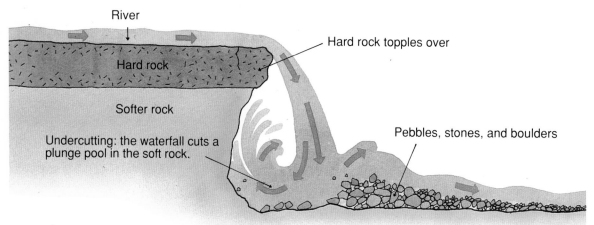

River

Hard rock

Hard rock topples over

Softer rock

Undercutting: the waterfall cuts a plunge pool in the soft rock.

Pebbles, stones, and boulders

Case Study

One of the most famous waterfalls in the world is Niagara Falls in North America. The Falls are partly in Canada and partly in the United States.

▼ Niagara Falls are visited each year by hundreds of thousands of tourists. Goat Island separates the American Falls in the United States from the Horseshoe Falls in Canada.

Horseshoe Falls

Niagara River

Goat Island

CANADA

◄——— To the Sir Adam Beck hydroelectric power station in Canada

- Angel Falls (3,212 ft) in Venezuela and Tugela Falls (3,110 ft) in South Africa are the world's highest waterfalls. Yosemite Falls (2,425 ft) is the highest in North America. Iguaçu Falls in South America spans more than 2 miles, making it the world's widest.

- The deepest gorge in the United States is Hells Canyon in the northwest. There the Snake River has cut a 40-mile-long gorge. It is more than 8,000 feet deep in places.

▶ The Grand Canyon, one of the most spectacular gorges in the world, is cut by the Colorado River in Arizona. The canyon is nearly 300 miles long, over 1 mile deep, and, in some places, nearly 18 miles wide.

Geography Detective

Draw a picture of the photograph of Niagara Falls. Draw arrows and write labels to show where you would expect to find: a plunge pool; a band of harder rock lying above softer rock; a gorge.

The colossal force of Niagara Falls has cut a deep valley, or gorge. The falls are retreating backward at a rate that ranges between three inches and six feet a year. If nothing is done to stop this, the waterfall will cut a valley the length of a football field in your lifetime.

The power of waterfalls like Niagara is often used to make hydroelectricity. Water from the river is chaneled to fall with great force down massive pipes to a power station below. The force of the falling water spins wheels that turn turbines, or engines. The turbines generate electricity.

When a River Bends

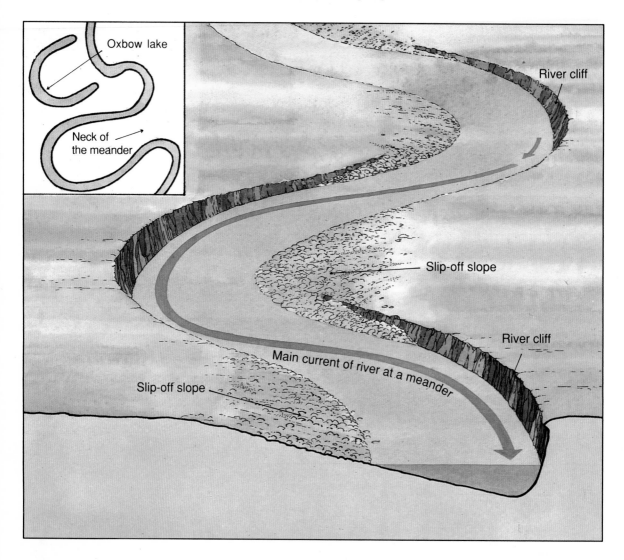

Oxbow lake

Neck of
the meander

River cliff

Slip-off slope

River cliff

Main current of river at a meander

Slip-off slope

Meanders, or bends, are often found where a valley floor is flat. This flat floor is called the **floodplain** of the river. It is flat because it is covered with thin layers of mud called **alluvium**. These layers are laid down each time the river floods over its banks. Fine particles of mud in the still water sink slowly to the ground like the dregs that collect at the bottom of a cup of coffee. Each time a river floods, it also leaves a layer of alluvium on its banks. Slowly, the banks become higher. These raised banks at the sides of a river are called **levees**.

▲ Bends in a river are called meanders. The force of water (the current) is greatest at the outside of the meander. It cuts into the bank here to form a **river cliff.** On the opposite bank, sand or pebbles pile up to form a feature called a **slip-off slope**. Here the current of the river is slow and weak, so it cannot carry sediment around the bend.

◄ These huge loops are meanders on the Okavango River, Botswana. When the river floods, it sometimes takes a shortcut, breaking through the narrow neck of a meander. The old meander left behind is called an **oxbow lake**.

● Meanders slow down river transport. Boats have to travel much farther when the river bends. Meanders can also be dangerous because of the shifts between fast and slow currents.

● Flooding has some benefits. Alluvium makes the land more fertile. And floodplains are flat, so they are easier to farm using machines.

Geography Detective

Durham, in England, is an old city whose cathedral and castle were built nearly 900 years ago. In this photograph, you can see these buildings stand on land that lies inside a meander of the Wear River.

In what ways is this part of Durham similar to an island? Why do you think this was a good place to build a castle?

When a River Floods

Case Study

A boy named Victor Heiser saw what happened at Johnstown, Pennsylvania, in 1889. He wrote: *My ears were stunned by the most terrifying noise I had ever heard in my sixteen years of life. I could see a huge wall advancing with incredible speed down the street. It was not recognizable as water. It was a dark mass in which seethed houses, wagons, trees, and animals. As this wall struck Washington Street broadside, my boyhood home was crushed like an eggshell before my eyes and I saw it disappear.*

Despite the most modern advances in engineering, rivers continue to flood. After weeks of heavy rain in June and July 1993, the Mississippi and its tributaries flooded their banks. Nearly 20

▲ The Johnstown flood in 1889 was a terrible disaster. More than 2,000 people died when days of heavy rain made the South Fork Dam crumble.

● The world's worst river flood took place in China. In September 1887, after weeks of heavy rain, the Huang River burst its banks. More than 1,500 towns and villages disappeared under floodwater and 1 million people died.

▶ Flooded homes near St. Louis, Missouri, in 1993.

● When the Nile floods each year, farmers build earthen walls to trap the floodwater. They use it to irrigate their crops. Without the Nile floods, fertile fields would soon turn back into desert.

million acres of farmland, 38,000 homes, and many roads and towns were damaged by the floodwaters.

Floods can even occur in dry lands. Sudden downpours in the Sahara Desert have caused torrents of water to rush through old valleys, drowning people who were camping there. River floods are also caused when snow and ice in high mountains melt rapidly. In southeast Asia, very strong seasonal, or **monsoon**, winds often bring heavy rain. Rivers then overflow their banks and cause serious flooding.

Geography Detective

Imagine that you are a television reporter and the picture on the screen is showing the floods near St. Louis, Missouri, in 1993. What will you tell viewers about the damage the flood has done to the land? What effect do you think it had on the people living there?

◀ In many parts of the world people depend on floodwater to grow their crops. These farmers in China are planting rice seedlings in a flooded paddy field. Rice is the only cereal crop that has to be grown in waterlogged soil.

Controlling the Flow of a River

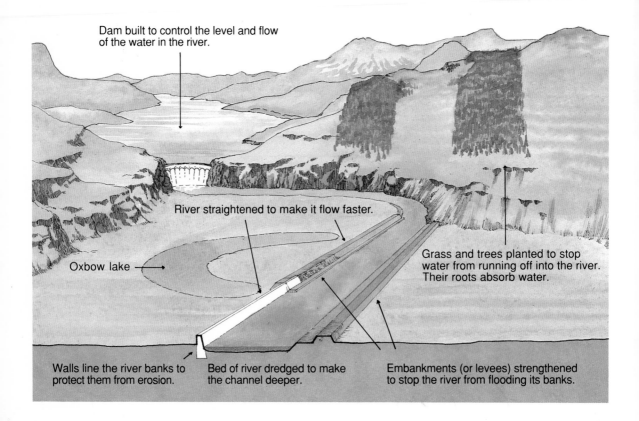

Dam built to control the level and flow of the water in the river.

River straightened to make it flow faster.

Oxbow lake

Grass and trees planted to stop water from running off into the river. Their roots absorb water.

Walls line the river banks to protect them from erosion.

Bed of river dredged to make the channel deeper.

Embankments (or levees) strengthened to stop the river from flooding its banks.

▲ River engineers use a number of different methods to control the flow of a river and to make it less likely to flood or damage its banks. In many cases, making the course of the river straighter and making the banks stronger will be enough.

Dams and **reservoirs**, or artificial lakes, help control the flow of water during a flood. They are often built on tributary streams rather than on the main river itself. When the water level starts to rise, the dams hold back the extra water, which is stored in the reservoir. The water is released later, when dry weather causes the main river level to fall.

Actions to protect land from flooding are called flood control measures. Damming a river means that a lake will spread in the valley behind the dam. This can have a devastating effect on people's lives and can harm wildlife. People will lose their

● The Tennessee Valley Authority (TVA) in Tennessee was started in the 1930s to prevent flooding and help people make better use of land. The TVA system covers an area of more than 39,000 square miles. It involved the construction of 50 dams and 40 hydroelectric power stations. When melting snow or heavy rain raises the river level, the dams hold back the extra water to stop it from flooding farms and fields.

18

In Berne, Switzerland, as in most cities, the flow of the river is carefully controlled. Walls protect the banks to stop the river from eroding them. A drop in river level has even been used to make hydroelectricity. The small lake formed behind the hydroelectric dam holds extra water when the river level rises.

homes, farms, and towns. The dam also disrupts the habits and travel patterns of fish and other wildlife. And the reservoir can affect the vegetation, changing the food supply for wildlife.

Geography Detective

This is a large outdoor working model of the Mississippi River system. The level of water is controlled to make it the same as on the real river system. If the measuring instruments show that the water level in a tributary river of the Mississippi has risen by two feet, for instance, the level of water in the model river can be raised by the same amount. How do you think a model like this can help river engineers deal with a flood? Will the model make it possible for them to warn people in time to protect their homes?

Dams and Reservoirs

◀ Lake Kariba is partly in Zambia and partly in Zimbabwe. It is the second largest artificial lake in Africa. The lake began to fill with water in 1961 after the Kariba Dam was built on the Zambezi River. Thousands of wild animals were trapped by the rising floodwaters until a mammoth rescue plan, *Operation Noah*, was put into effect. Game wardens, using boats, took many animals to safety.

Reservoirs such as Lake Kariba supply people in most countries with fresh water. In dry areas, dams also store water to irrigate farmland. In countries with many deep valleys, such as Norway and Japan, dams are built to store water for generating hydroelectricity.

Case Study

Australia is a dry land. One of its few reliable sources of water is the Snowy Mountains drainage system. The rivers here are filled with melting snow and heavy rainfall. To make the best use of this water, engineers tunneled through a mountain to change the course of the Snowy River. They built 16 dams to store water in reservoirs. The largest of these is Lake Eucumbene. Much

▼ Part of the Snowy Mountains hydroelectric power project in southeastern Australia.

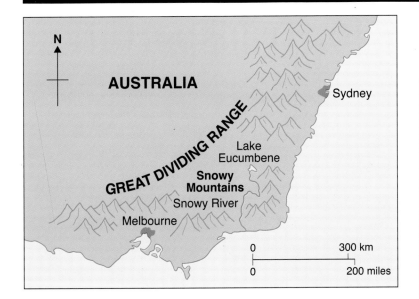

AUSTRALIA

N

GREAT DIVIDING RANGE

Sydney

Lake
Eucumbene

**Snowy
Mountains**

Snowy River

Melbourne

| 0 | 300 km |
| 0 | 200 miles |

◀ This map of Australia shows the position of the Snowy Mountain drainage system.

● Sometimes problems arise when people from different countries share the same river system. When water is taken for irrigation, the flow of a river is reduced. Much of the irrigation water evaporates instead of flowing back into the river. This can make life difficult for people living farther down the valley. They have less fresh water for household use and for irrigation. Shallower water may make it difficult for boats to use the river.

of the stored water is used to irrigate a very large area of farmland. Eight power stations also generate hydroelectricity for Sydney and Melbourne, Australia's largest cities.

● The most powerful hydroelectric power station in the world is at Itaipu on the Paraná River in South America. It will soon be overtaken by the Tunguska River project in Russia.

Geography Detective

Copy or trace this picture. Imagine that you are a river engineer. Where would you build a dam to supply fresh water to a nearby city? Draw in your dam on your copy of the picture and show how the reservoir will look when the dam has been built.

Using Rivers for Transportation

◀ This is a river port at Chongqing in China. More than 3 million people live in this important Asian city. It is situated on the banks of the Chang River. Boats sailing to the seaport of Shanghai from here have about 1,500 miles to go before they reach the sea.

Many important ports are situated along the world's great rivers. Some **river ports**, like Baton Rouge and New Orleans on the Mississippi, are close to the river mouth. Other ports on the same river, such as St. Louis, are deep inside the United States. Rivers provide shelter for seagoing ships and a cheap and easy route into the heart of a country. This is especially important in areas such as the Amazon Basin, where the dense tropical rainforest makes it difficult to build roads and railways. The Brazilian river port of Manaus, for example, provides a shipping base in the Amazon Basin more than 1,000 miles from the sea.

Some rivers are difficult to navigate. Waterfalls, dams, wide meanders, hidden mudbanks, swift currents, floods, or low water make many rivers unsuitable for use as waterways.

Case Study

River transport is slower than road transport, but it is usually much cheaper. It is possible to take goods up the Rhine from Rotterdam in the

● Wide rivers can cause problems for land transport. It may be difficult for goods and passengers to cross to the other side. Cars and trucks may have to travel many miles along a river's banks to reach a crossing point, such as a bridge or a ferry.

● Using rivers for transport can have disadvantages. For example, leaking oil and litter from barges and steamers pollutes the water.

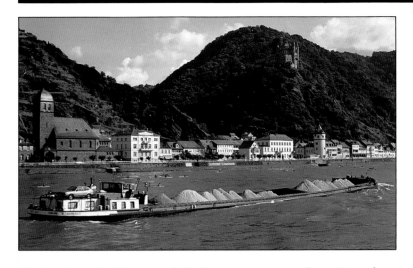

◀ Goods such as coal, iron ore, gravel (seen here), and timber are carried by barges on the Rhine. This is Europe's busiest inland waterway for shipping and for transportation.

Netherlands (the world's largest seaport) to Basel in Switzerland. Canals in Germany also link the Rhine with the Danube. Goods can travel by water all the way from Rotterdam to the Black Sea ports of Russia, or to Istanbul in Turkey.

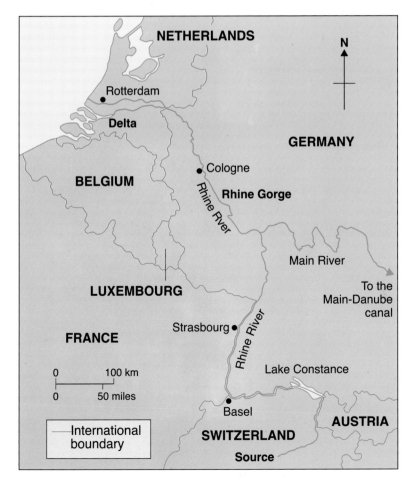

This map shows the Rhine waterway. Rivers such as the Rhine help transportation in two ways. Goods can be carried by water, and river valleys provide a flat surface for roads and railways.

Geography Detective

Use the photograph of the Rhine barge to draw a picture. Use arrows and labels to name the main features of a Rhine barge: the hold where the cargo is stored; the type of cargo; the control room; the living quarters of the captain and family. What clue makes it seem likely that this barge is their permanent home?

Using Rivers for Recreation

Rivers and streams are used today for many different types of recreation. People living a long way from the sea, including many Americans and Russians, use rivers and lakes for swimming, rowing, sailing, canoeing, waterskiing, windsurfing, and fishing.

● Rivers also attract vacationers. More than 4 million tourists visit the Grand Canyon in the United States each year. Other river sightseeing attractions in the world include Victoria Falls on the Zambezi in Africa, the Rhine Gorge in Europe, Angel Falls in Venezuela (South America) and the sacred Ganges River in India (Asia).

● Using rivers for recreation has disadvantages. Fuel from motorboats and riverboat cruises pollutes the water. Swimmers and boaters disturb wildlife.

▲ This picture shows people whitewater rafting on the Colorado River in the United States. As fast-flowing water passes over rocks on the river bed, the water foams and turns white at the surface. Canoeing and kayaking are other whitewater sports.

▶ This luxury cruise ship is on the Nile at Luxor in Egypt. The passengers sleep in cabins and enjoy meals cooked on board. They sail from Cairo up the Nile to see the monuments of ancient Egypt. The journey takes several days.

▶ These children are fishing for food with large baskets in Bangladesh. Fishing is a popular sport but it is also an important source of food in many countries.

◀ In India, many people follow the Hindu religion. They believe that the Ganges is a sacred river. Here people are bathing in the Ganges at the Hindus' holy city, Varanasi.

Geography Detective

What rivers are close to your home? Are any of them used for boating, swimming, or fishing? Are any rivers near you scenic spots, places to picnic by, or places to enjoy a walk along a trail?

River Wildlife

The insects, birds, fish, mammals, and other animals living in or near the world's rivers all depend on plants for their food. Even the creatures that do not eat plants eat other creatures that do. For example, an antelope eats grass and then a lion comes along and eats the antelope. Salmon eat small plant-eating fish but are themselves eaten by bears and by birds of prey. In this way animals all depend on plants and on each other for their food. This is called a food chain.

▼ This swampy river valley is in the tropical grasslands of Tanzania in Africa. The valley is home to many kinds of wildlife.

◀ A brown bear and its cub in the Brooks River, Alaska.

▼ This Mata Mata turtle is on the banks of the Amazon River, in the tropical rainforests of South America.

● Human actions affect the places where animals live. Dams prevent fish from swimming upstream. This is one reason why the number of wild salmon has fallen rapidly in recent years.

● Pollution of rivers by sewage, fertilizers, pesticides, and other waste products is another way in which humans affect wildlife. Some rivers are so polluted that they are considered dead. Neither fish nor plants can live there.

◀ This salmon ladder is beside a hydroelectric dam. The pools are made with concrete, and the water has artificial currents in it. The ladder helps some salmon swim upstream to lay their eggs. Young salmon start life in the gravel beds of mountain streams. Then they swim down to the ocean, where they spend most of their adult life. At the end of their life, salmon return to the stream where they were born. There they spawn, then die.

Different types of plants need different amounts of sunshine, warmth, and rainfall. These are the main reasons why the plants that grow along the banks of rivers in northern Canada are not the same as those in the rainforests of South America or in the swamps of eastern Africa. The types of fish, insects, birds, and animals that can live and feed there are also different. Each type of environment has its own set of plants and wildlife. This is called a habitat.

Geography Detective

This river in Saarland, Germany, has been polluted with chemicals. The fish are dead.

Make a list of some of the things that pollute rivers and harm the plants and wildlife living there. How can we protect rivers in order to preserve plants, fish, and other river creatures?

Mapwork

This map shows the valley of the Big River. As you can see, it flows into a lake.

1. Use a ruler and the scale on the map to find the length of the Big River. Take a straight line from its source to its mouth.
2. Use the scale on the map to find how far a fish would travel if it swam the complete length of the Big River from its source to its mouth. Use a length of string or thread to follow all the bends in the course of the river. What is the difference between this distance and the distance in a straight line?
3. In which general direction does the Big River flow from its source to its mouth? Use the compass in the lower left corner of the map to find out.
4. Make a copy of the map. Find the features on the map that are similar to those shown in the three photographs. Write in the names of these features in the empty boxes on the map.
5. On your copy of the map, write W, T, or P to show a place where you would expect to see
   a) a lot of workers (mark it with the letter W);
   b) traffic crossing the Big River (mark it with the letter T);
   c) a stretch of the river that may be polluted (mark it with the letter P).

▲ Meander

▲ Delta

▲ Waterfall

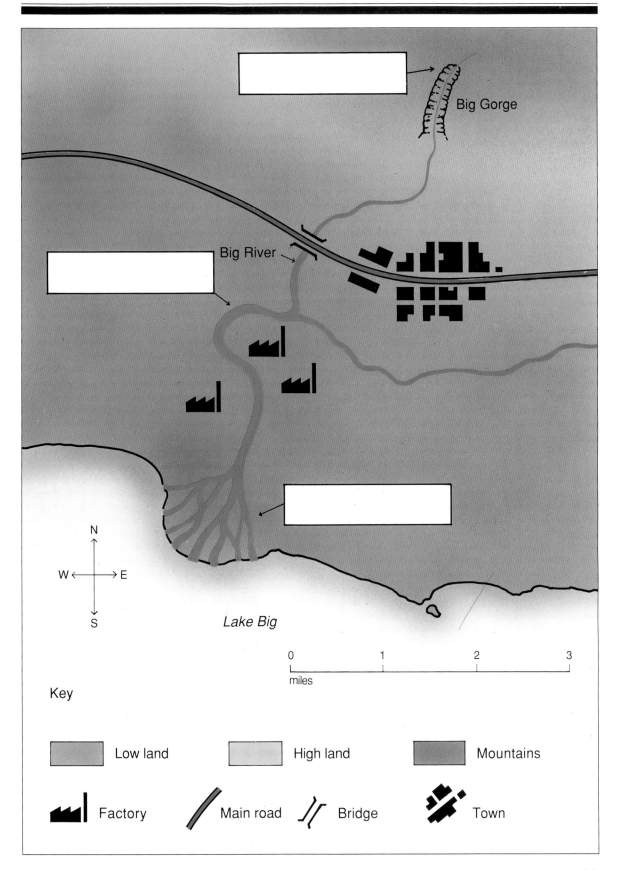

Big Gorge

Big River

N
W ← → E
S

Lake Big

0   1   2   3
miles

Key

	Low land		High land		Mountains

Factory   Main road   Bridge   Town

Glossary

alluvium: The fine mud or silt left by a river on its floodplain.

confluence: The place where one river joins another, or where two rivers merge into one.

delta: A fan-shaped deposit at the mouth of a river. It divides the river into many smaller channels. It is named after the triangular shape of the Greek letter delta Δ.

deposit: Mud, sand, and pebbles dropped (deposited) on the bottom of a river, a lake, or the sea.

distributary: A channel in a delta. When a river deposits sediment that blocks the flow of the water, it then divides into smaller channels, or distributaries.

drainage basin: The area of land drained by a river and its tributaries.

drainage system: The network of waterways formed by a river and its tributaries.

equator: The imaginary line drawn on maps around the center of the earth.

erode: To wear down earth or rocks by the action of water, wind, or ice.

estuary: A river mouth in which salt water from ocean tides mixes with the river's fresh water.

evaporate: To change water from a liquid to an invisible gas called water vapor.

floodplain: The flat, fertile valley floor of a river. The floodplain is formed by the river repeatedly flooding its banks, causing sediment to settle on the ground.

gorge: A steep-sided river valley. Many gorges are formed by waterfalls.

hydroelectricity: Electricity generated from waterpower.

irrigate: To provide crops with extra water to help them grow.

levee: The natural bank of a river, built up each time a river floods its banks and deposits sediment. Sometimes people build levees up even higher to help prevent flooding.

meander: A bend in the course of a river.

monsoon: A strong seasonal wind that brings heavy rain at the same time each year, primarily in Asian countries.

mouth: The point where a river enters a larger river, a lake, or the sea.

oxbow lake: A lake that is made when a river takes a "shortcut" across the narrow neck of a meander that has bent into a nearly complete loop.

pothole: A round hole in a river bed, often at the base of a waterfall. The hole is formed by pebbles that are swirled around by fast-flowing water.

reservoir: An artificial lake in which people store water for later use.

river cliff: A cliff formed by the strong current in a river as it erodes the bank on the outside bend of a meander.

river port: A town on the banks of a river where there are safe places for barges, boats, or ships to dock and be loaded or unloaded with goods.

runoff: Water that does not soak into the ground but runs into a river, lake, or ocean.

sediment: Mud, sand, or broken shells and stones that are carried along by water, then deposited.

slip-off slope: A gentle slope on the inside bend of a meander, where the river current is at its weakest and sediment is deposited.

source: The start of a river.

spring: The point where underground water comes to the surface.

tributary: A river that joins a larger river.

water cycle: The endless process of water evaporating from the sea, forming clouds, falling as rain, then flowing back to the sea and evaporating again.

waterfall: A sudden drop in height in the flow of a river.

watershed: The line separating one drainage system from another. The term can also refer to a drainage basin.

wetland: A marsh, swamp, or other low, wet area that often borders a river, lake, or ocean.

METRIC CONVERSION CHART		
WHEN YOU KNOW	**MULTIPLY BY**	**TO FIND**
inches	25.4	millimeters
inches	2.54	centimeters
feet	0.3048	meters
miles	1.609	kilometers
square miles	2.59	square kilometers
acres	0.4047	hectares
gallons	3.78	liters
degrees Fahrenheit	.56 (after subtracting 32)	degrees Celsius

Index